# Half Sentences

poems stitched from ordinary moments

Nitya Pal

/ BookLeaf
Publishing
India | USA | UK

Made with ❤ on the BookLeaf Publishing Platform

www.bookleafpub.in

www.bookleafpub.com

# Dedication

for the people who stayed when i rambled,
and for the people who left mid-sentence
both taught me how to write this book.

# Preface

i never planned to write a book.

i was just collecting little moments

like notes in the margins, things we forget to say out loud.

half sentences is not about perfect poems.

it's about the kind of things we laugh about, complain about, or think about when no one's watching.

if you've ever stared at a loading screen too long, or kept a thought unfinished on purpose:

you'll find yourself here.

# Acknowledgements

thanks to everyone who laughed with me in cafeterias,
who shared playlists on long bus rides,
who sent random links, shared little jokes, passed notes
in class,
or kept me company in the quietest ways and
who reminded me that poetry lives in small things.
and to the strangers who will hold these pages
thank you for meeting me halfway,
between the lines.

# 1. capslock off

capslock off feels like
writing a note in pencil,
knowing the smudge
is part of its charm.

it's whispering secrets
to the fridge light at midnight,
or folding laundry
to the rhythm of your own hum.

capslock off feels like
switching the room lights low,
not because you're sad,
but because soft lamps
make the evening sweeter.

capslock off is
talking in lowercase laughter,
leaving voice notes with background rain,
saving memes at 2 a.m.
like little postcards
you'll send your future self.

capslock off is when

the world stops being a headline,
and becomes a scribble in the margin
a dog's tail hitting the floor,
a stranger holding the door,
your playlist shuffling into the perfect song
right when you need it.

some lives are lived
in exclamation marks,
but mine?
i like the commas
the slow breath,
the steady pause,
the lowercase kind of love.

# 2. the void

the void is that second
after you press "send" on an email
and remember the typo in line one.

it's the space between
your phone slipping off the bed
and hitting the floor
heartbeat included.

the void is standing in the shower
trying to remember
if you already shampooed once
or just imagined it.

it's scrolling to the end of a recipe blog,
only to find ten paragraphs of life story
before the ingredients show up.

the void is the limbo
between skip ad in 5 seconds
and realizing five seconds
has never felt longer.

and yes,

the void is netflix asking,
are you still watching?
when both of you know
the answer is always yes.

because in the end,
the void is just that
the blank pause,
the empty stretch,
the little nothing
we all end up filling
with our own noise.

# 3. i am the poem

i am the poem
you didn't know you were reading,
the line that caught in your throat,
the comma you almost skipped.

i am spilled ink
on a page that no one asked for,
a breath between verses,
a word left unsaid
that matters anyway.

i am small moments
the mug you lift without thinking,
the streetlamp glowing in rain,
the laugh that escapes
before your mind catches it.

i am the poem
and so are you.
we are every little stanza
we live,
we stumble through,
we survive.

# 4. delulu

they laughed at my wild plans,
the ones i whispered at 2 a.m.,
the ones scribbled in notebook margins
that make no sense to anyone else.

delulu, they said.
maybe i am
i imagine apartments i'll never rent,
write letters to people who won't reply,
dream of moments
that probably don't exist.

but in the middle of it,
i feel alive.
i feel hope.
i feel colors
that the world in daylight
can't see.

maybe being delulu
is not losing touch
but finding pieces of yourself
hidden in impossible dreams.

# 5. ghosted by god

been praying lately,
but it feels like the texts aren't delivering.
read receipts off,
divine typing bubble gone.

i light a candle,
wait for a sign,
get a power cut instead.
maybe that *is* the sign.

my mom says "have faith,"
but faith's been quiet lately,
like a friend who said "we'll meet soon"
and never sent the location.

maybe god's just busy
or letting me figure it out myself
like when you stop helping a kid
with the puzzle they keep messing up.

still,
every time things somehow work out,
i smile a little

like okay; maybe
the message did go through after all.

# 6. undo

i wish life had a shortcut key,
like ctrl+z when you trip on a word
or send that text too soon.

undo the moment i hit "reply all"
when i only meant one person,
undo the time i waved back
to someone who wasn't waving at me.

undo the way i rehearsed a joke all day,
then forgot the punchline mid-laugh,
undo the time autocorrect betrayed me
with words i never meant to send.

but then again,
if every slip could be erased,
wouldn't we lose the stories
we tell years later,
how mistakes became
the funniest parts of us?

# 7. autoplay

i said "just one video,"
but the algorithm knows me
better than i know myself.

suddenly it's 3:17 a.m.
and i'm watching a raccoon
flip pancakes in slow motion,
while the "next up" preview
is already rolling.

i let episodes stack like dirty dishes,
another cliffhanger,
another "previously on"
that i barely remember living through.

autoplay is sneaky like that.
one minute you're in control,
the next it's deciding for you,
whispering, "stay a little longer."

life feels like that sometimes too,
you blink,
and another chapter starts,
whether you are ready or not.

# 8. happy is hot

happiness isn't quiet.
it's dancing in your room
with hair still wet from the shower,
laughing so hard
you almost drop your phone,
ordering dessert
just because.

happy is hot
like a song on repeat
that makes you walk faster,
like sunshine on your skin
when you weren't planning
to go outside,
like the confidence that comes
from wearing your favorite outfit
on an ordinary tuesday.

happy is hot
not perfect, not polished,
but alive.
and when you let it spill out
messy, contagious,
a little louder than planned

everyone near you
feels warmer too.

# 9. plot twist

i thought today would be ordinary
coffee on the balcony,
emails answered,
the bus on time.

then the cat knocked over my mug,
the bus broke down,
and a stranger smiled at me
just when i needed it most.

life loves plot twists
small, quiet ones
that change nothing on paper
but everything inside.

sometimes it's a wrong turn
that leads to the best street food,
a delayed train
that shows you the sunset,
a forgotten book
that turns out to hold the exact line
you needed.

plot twist isn't drama,

it's the tiny miracles
we don't script but somehow survive.

# 10. update available

the screen lights up
"update available."
i swipe it away,
again, again, again.

not today.
not when I'm tired.
not when change feels heavier
than the life I already carry.

but later, i wonder
if people came with updates,
would mine read:
less scared to speak first?
bug fixes in confidence?
can finally rest without guilt?

maybe we are all running
on outdated versions,
still glitching with old fears,
still stalling at new beginnings.

and maybe
choosing to grow

isn't about pressing install.
it's about waking up one day
and realizing you already have.

# 11. recess

remember school bells?
the way 40 minutes of algebra
melted away
with one loud clang
recess.

life still has bells,
we just don't listen:
your friend texting "let's go get chai,"
your mom calling you for dinner,
the way laughter interrupts
a long, tired evening.

we keep waiting for vacations,
for weekends,
for someday.
but recess was never someday,
it was stolen in the middle of chaos.

i think life wants us
to still run to the canteen,
still sit on cold steps with snacks,
still forget the math problems for a while
before heading back,

lighter, not lonelier.

recess isn't over.
it's hidden in our days.
we just have to hear the bell.

# 12. chewing gum

you reach under the desk,
thinking maybe you'll find a pen cap
instead:
squish.

someone's leftover gum,
probably older than the school itself,
now your finger's
unwanted souvenir.

the teacher's explaining photosynthesis,
you're stuck wondering
who in this class had strawberry orbit
and zero shame.

it's disgusting,
but also
a weird kind of autograph,
proof someone was here before you.

maybe that's life:
we all leave gum somewhere,
not polished, not pretty
just traces that stick.

# 13. earphones

every pair i buy,
turns into a magician.
one month in
poof! left ear disappears.
the wire knots itself overnight,
like it's auditioning for yoga.

borrowed from a friend?
return it
one side already gone,
and somehow, it's my fault.
apparently, i cursed it.

even bluetooth ones
they fall out mid-run,
and i'm chasing them down the street
like they're toddlers escaping a fair.

but still,
that moment when both sides work,
full volume, favorite song
the world feels conquerable.
maybe life is also like earphones:
not perfect, sometimes half silent,

but worth it for those minutes
when the music is whole.

# 14. sticky notes on fridge

yellow squares everywhere,
like the fridge caught chickenpox.
"buy milk."
"call dadi."
"stop stealing mangoes."

one falls off every time the door slams,
slipping under the microwave,
where it waits
to be rediscovered months later
a fossil of good intentions.

the notes outlive the food inside:
milk sours, bread molds,
but "don't forget dentist"
still stares at you
six weeks late.

maybe sticky notes
aren't reminders for the chores
they're reminders
that we keep trying to hold life
with little squares of paper.

# 15. ringtone in library

dead silence,
pages flipping like whispers,
and then
"jalebi baiiiii, jalebi baiiiii"

the owner panics,
hands shaking,
phone slips twice before
finally pressing decline.

everyone staring,
trying not to laugh,
because it could've been us
it has been us.

once it was nokia tune,
once "baby baby baby ohhh,"
always something embarrassing,
always louder than it should be.

and maybe that's life:
you spend years trying to look composed,
but your ringtone betrays you
reminding the world you're still human.

# 16. barefoot & okay

i kick off my shoes in the living room,
the carpet tickles my toes,
the laundry basket tilts like it's about to fall
but i don't care.

barefoot & okay
because the mail came late again,
the milk expired,
the dishes piled up,
and i still sit cross-legged on the floor,
laughing at a meme
i already saw this morning.

it's in the little rebellions:
stepping into cold kitchen tiles,
singing in the shower
when no one can hear,
touching the soft spot on a book
that belonged to someone who isn't here.

i realize:
i don't need to have it figured out,
just solid ground,
a sound that feels like me,

and room to breathe.

barefoot & okay
is a whisper to myself:
you've walked through storms,
you've stumbled over cracks,
you've lingered in silence,
and yet
here you are,
still soft,
still human,
still okay.

# 17. captcha

click the images with traffic lights
i squint at the corner,
is that a pole?
why does proving i'm human
make me feel like a machine?

box after box,
check after check,
a silent quiz i never studied for,
but somehow always pass,
barely.

the irony:
a bot trying to look like me,
me trying not to look like a bot.
who's really convincing whom?

patience runs thinner
with each blurry pixel,
until i almost forget
what page i wanted to open.

and maybe that's the point:
life is also a captcha,

a series of boxes to tick,
just to prove to someone,
or maybe to myself,
that i belong.

# 18. instant noodles

three minutes is a lifetime
when your stomach growls louder
than the kettle's whistle.
boiling water turns heroic,
steam rising like a tiny volcano.

sometimes i forget the sachet,
sometimes i pour two,
sometimes it's gourmet,
other times it's cardboard,
but always, it's dinner.

late-night hostels,
one spoon shared by four,
someone steals an extra slurp
friendship measured in broth
and cheap laughter.

even fancy feasts
can't compete with
crouching by the stove,
watching noodles soften
like an opening fist.

maybe that's why
they taste like home:
comfort that waits in packets,
reminding us
life doesn't need fine dining,
just hot water and patience.

# 19. archive

somewhere in my phone,
buried between bank messages
and food delivery receipts,
is a graveyard of photos
that no one else remembers.

screenshots of tweets,
half-written drafts,
that one meme i swore
i'd send later
never did.

folders named "final"
and "final 2" and "final final,"
like i was archiving
versions of myself
that never quite finished loading.

the weirdest part?
i never look at them,
yet i can't delete them.
as if each pixel
is a breadcrumb trail back to me.

maybe archives aren't for revisiting.
maybe they exist to prove
that we once cared enough
to press save
even on things we'd outgrow.

# 20. 404

i looked everywhere
in the drawer, under the bed,
in my old notebooks,
the photo i swore i saved.

404. not found.

it's the quiet ache of misplacing yourself,
the way memories hide
just when you need them.

i check my messages,
my old emails,
hoping someone, somewhere
has a breadcrumb
leading back to me.

sometimes the search ends in frustration.
sometimes it ends in laughter.
sometimes 404
is not loss,
but a reminder
that you are still looking,
and that is enough.

# 21. the last page of notebook

the handwriting is always bigger here,
like i suddenly stopped caring
about straight lines.

doodles fill the corners
a spaceship,
someone's initials,
a cat that looks nothing like a cat.

half equations i never solved,
song lyrics from a romantic playlist,
a phone number that doesn't exist anymore.

i even play tic-tac-toe with myself,
losing both sides,
winning nothing but time.

the last page never asks
for perfect endings,
only proof that i was here,
scribbling life in the margins.

# 22. don't tell mom

we spilled coke on the carpet again,
threw a cushion over it,
like that fixes anything.
the ceiling fan keeps spinning
pretending it didn't see a thing.

there's a half-eaten paratha in the sink,
a cracked plate under the sofa,
someone's homework drying
on the balcony rail.
we're professionals at disaster management.

don't tell mom
about the nail polish on the tiles,
or the pizza bill still in the bin,
or how we reheated the roti
three times before eating.

we laughed till the bulb flickered,
till the neighbour's dog started barking,
till we forgot what started it all.
for a minute
it felt like freedom had our surname.

but when the night softens,
we still tiptoe past her room,
still keep the TV volume low,
still whisper "just five more minutes,"
like bedtime is a law we can bend.

and i think:
maybe growing up
isn't learning the rules
it's learning which ones
to break softly,
and still get away with it.